This book belongs to :

....

NOAH'S ARK

PUBLISHED BY PETER HADDOCK LIMITED,
BRIDLINGTON, ENGLAND
PRINTED IN ITALY

ISBN 07105 0240 0

Since their creation men gradually became worse in their behaviour and their sinfulness was evident in all their actions. There were wars and fights daily and when God looked down on the earth. He regretted having created man. He decided to destroy the entire humanity by sinking the earth with the water of the Deluge.

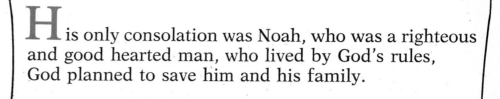

His only consolation was Noah, who was a righteous and good hearted man, who lived by God's rules, God planned to save him and his family.

One day, while Noah was working in his vineyard, God sent a dove to speak
to Noah in His name. God said unto Noah, "I am going to destroy all living
creatures because the earth is filled with evil and violence. But you, Noah,
and your wife, and your sons, Shem, Ham, and Japheth, and their wives will be saved.
This is a promise I make to you, Noah, a promise which will be called a covenant.
The earth will be destroyed by a great flood, therefore, I command you to build
a large boat of cypress wood which will be known as an ark."

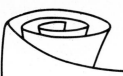

Noah returned to his house and told his family how God had spoken to him. He explained why they had been selected by God and how they were to build an ark to save the human race and the animals.

The ark had to be large enough to hold two animals of each species, a male and female, and themselves. They would, therefore, have to start work immediately.

Noah and his family began to build the ark according to God's instructions, with three floors, a window, a roof, and a door in the side. The ark was to be seventy-five feet wide and forty-five feet high and sealed with pitch both inside and out, so that no water could enter.

Noah would check the progress of the ark daily, making sure that God's instructions were being followed.

Finally the day came when the ark was ready and Noah, together with all his relatives, was at last able to admire with great satisfaction the result of their efforts. All the many hours of toil they had spent each day had created the ark, which was exactly according to what God had ordered. Noah had obeyed the command of God and the ark stood in magnificent splendour ready to be boarded.

Obedient as always, Noah followed God's orders and commenced the task of gathering all the animals together. Two animals of every species, one male and one female, God had said, and this was what Noah collected, no matter how large or how small the creature may be, no creature was overlooked by Noah.

At last when all the animals had been gathered together they began to enter the ark, two by two, until all were safe inside. There were tigers and giraffes, monkeys and oxen, zebras and eagles, elephants and ants, and birds of every colour and kind. Noah's grandchildren had never before seen so many animals assembled together.

When all the animals were safely aboard, Noah gathered together his sons and their families. They took aboard with them the food which was to provide nourishment for the many occupants during the long period they were to spend aboard the ark. Noah had prepared the ark well, there was grass and hay for the animals to sleep on and plenty of room for everyone, all the animals were able to live together in peace and freedom. The food, along with the many other necessities, was safely stored away in the ark.

Finally, Noah's family closed and locked the door of the huge ark. They then waited for a sign that the flood had begun, but for six days nothing happened. After seven days had passed, according to God's word, it started to rain. Outside the sky turned a bleak grey and water poured from the heavens, the great Deluge had begun.

For forty days and forty nights it rained, day after day without interruption. As the great oceans and rivers overflowed, the water rose and rose until all the valleys and fields were flooded with water.

The rain continued to fall on the earth both day and night, never ceasing but pouring down relentlessly. Higher, higher and higher the flood rose until everything on earth was beneath the water, even the highest mountain was submerged below the great waters.

Men, animals and the wicked things of the world were swallowed up by the dark waves and sucked beneath the murky water. Only Noah and his companions aboard the ark remained alive and safe in their sanctuary as God had foretold.

They had a great deal to do aboard the ark each day, the animals had to be fed and watered, as Noah had to ensure that all the animals aboard survived the journey to prevent the extinction of any of the creatures of the earth, because these animals were to be the only survivors.

During this time Noah studied the animals and soon became familiar with their ways and gained a great knowledge of all aboard. Trusting in God, who would help them to survive, Noah became even more wise and patient than before.

As the days passed by, the rain continued to fall and the sky continued to get darker, an infinite storm which never ceased. On and on it raged for days and days as God had promised, ridding the world of all its evil. All aboard the ark were safe, but they did not know if the storm would ever subside, or whether, in fact, God had deserted them, so condemming them to live the rest of their lives aboard the great boat.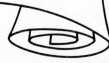

Noah's grandchildren loved the animals, as all children do, and would often help Noah to feed them. Noah took the opportunity to explain to the children how well organised and complete the life of the animals was, even the smallest creatures such as the bees and the ants. Great was the knowledge of Noah.

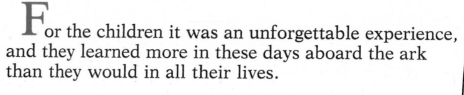

For the children it was an unforgettable experience, and they learned more in these days aboard the ark than they would in all their lives.

Finally, after having rained for forty days and forty nights, the rain stopped and the sky cleared. The great storm was over. For one hundred and fifty days they floated on a vast ocean till finally God sent a wind to blow upon the earth, and slowly the water began to recede. Eventually the ark came to rest on a mountain, which was called Ararat in Mesopotamia.

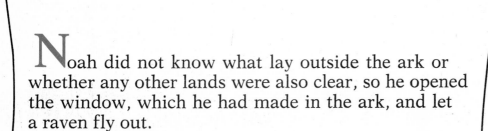
Noah did not know what lay outside the ark or whether any other lands were also clear, so he opened the window, which he had made in the ark, and let a raven fly out.

Noah watched the bird fly away, far out over the waters. The bird flew to and fro, searching for land, but did not return to Noah in his ark.

Noah then released a white dove asking it to return as soon as possible to tell him of its findings and with proof that the earth was safe again.

Many hours passed and Noah feared that the dove would not return, but at last the dove appeared and in its beak was a freshly plucked green olive leaf.

Noah rejoiced in the knowledge that other lands were now clear of the water and believed that these lands were not far away.

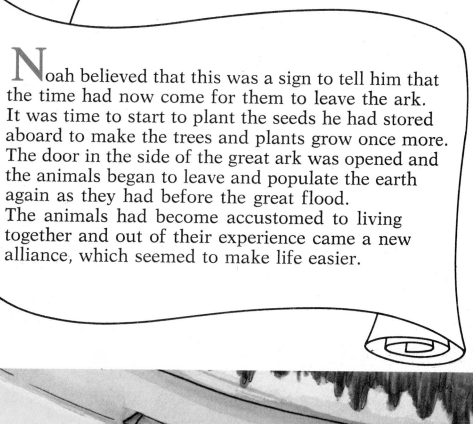

Noah believed that this was a sign to tell him that the time had now come for them to leave the ark. It was time to start to plant the seeds he had stored aboard to make the trees and plants grow once more. The door in the side of the great ark was opened and the animals began to leave and populate the earth again as they had before the great flood.

The animals had become accustomed to living together and out of their experience came a new alliance, which seemed to make life easier.

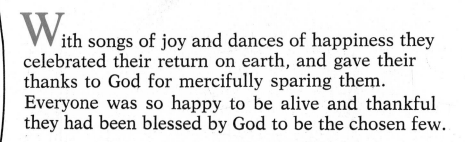

With songs of joy and dances of happiness they celebrated their return on earth, and gave their thanks to God for mercifully sparing them. Everyone was so happy to be alive and thankful they had been blessed by God to be the chosen few.

God then used his mighty powers and created a rainbow, which was new to the earth as one had never before been sighted. The rainbow was the sign of the new alliance between God and the creatures of the earth, a token of the everlasting covenant. Never again would He send a Deluge to destroy man and the rainbow was present as a sign of His indulgence. From Noah, and from his sons, Shem, Ham and Japheth, would grow the new lineage of the earth.